-»» Start «««-
something
good

THE QUAKER COOKBOOK

PENGUIN
ENTERPRISE

PENGUIN ENTERPRISE
Published by the Penguin Group
Penguin Books India Pvt. Ltd, 7th Floor, Infinity Tower C, DLF Cyber City,
Gurgaon 122 002, Haryana, India
Penguin Group (USA) Inc., 375 Hudson Street, New York, New York 10014, USA
Penguin Group (Canada), 90 Eglinton Avenue East, Suite 700, Toronto,
Ontario, M4P 2Y3, Canada
Penguin Books Ltd, 80 Strand, London WC2R 0RL, England
Penguin Ireland, 25 St Stephen's Green, Dublin 2, Ireland (a division of Penguin Books Ltd)
Penguin Group (Australia), 707 Collins Street, Melbourne, Victoria 3008, Australia
Penguin Group (NZ), 67 Apollo Drive, Rosedale, Auckland 0632, New Zealand
Penguin Books (South Africa) (Pty) Ltd, Block D, Rosebank Office Park, 181 Jan
Smuts Avenue, Parktown North, Johannesburg 2193, South Africa

Penguin Books Ltd, Registered Offices: 80 Strand, London WC2R 0RL, England

First published in Penguin Enterprise by Penguin Books India 2015
Penguin Enterprise is the custom publishing imprint of Penguin Books India

10 9 8 7 6 5 4 3 2 1

ISBN 9780143424598

For sale in the Indian Subcontinent only

Photographs by Smita Srivastava
Design by BBDO INDIA PVT. LTD.
Printed at Replika Press Pvt. Ltd, India

A PENGUIN RANDOM HOUSE COMPANY

Introduction

Give your family wholesome, nourishing and tasty meals every day by simply adding **Quaker Oats.**

With its rich texture and neutral flavour, Quaker Oats can be used as an ingredient to enhance every dish, adding tasty goodness to all your meals.

Explore your culinary creativity through our recipe book and discover how **Quaker Oats** can be used every day to prepare almost any kind of dish from breakfast to desserts, from traditional Indian to continental and much much more.

At **Quaker,** we encourage you to experiment with the dishes you love by adding the tasty goodness of Quaker Oats to your favourite recipes.

So, go ahead and enjoy your family's compliments on the tasty food you create; while you feel good knowing that you've brought healthy goodness into their daily mealtimes by making *Everyday a Quaker day!*

We'd love to hear about your delicious dishes and what your family thought of them, so do share them with us at **www.facebook.com/QuakerIndia.**

Quaker Oats are for Everyday Goodness

Upma

Pear Crisp

Tomato Rice

Dosa

Mango Pancake

Suggested garnish

Discover the Power of
Quaker Oats-Supergrains

Our body needs energy to help keep us going. Wholegrains provide energy and are a source of dietary fibre. Quaker Oats is a wholegrain. It consists of oat endosperm, oat bran and oat germ.

Compared to most wholegrains, oats are higher in protein and healthy fats, and contain both insoluble and soluble dietary fibre.

Quaker Oats is good for the entire family!

OAT BRAN

contains the greatest amount of β-glucan, and is a rich source of B vitamins and nutrients, including trace minerals.

OAT GERM

is the heart of the grain and the smallest part of the kernel, but it is loaded with nutrients like B vitamins, vitamin E, trace minerals and phytochemicals.

OAT ENDOSPERM

is the largest section and middle layer. It serves as the main energy source of the plant, in the form of carbohydrate and protein.

Table of Contents

Quaker Appetizers, Salads and Soups

Quaker Oats Beet & Tomato Soup

Suggested garnishing.

Ingredients

- ½ cup Quaker Oats,* lightly roasted and powdered
- 4–5 ripe tomatoes, halved
- 1 medium-sized beet, roughly chopped
- 1 carrot, roughly chopped
- 2–3 cloves
- 4 peppercorns
- 4–5 garlic cloves, minced
- 1 onion, finely chopped
- ½ tsp dried rosemary
- 2 drops of oil
- Salt and pepper to taste

Preparation

- Heat 2 drops of oil in a pressure cooker. Sautè onion, herbs and spices till the onions turn pink.
- Add vegetables and 2½ cups of water.
- Pressure-cook for 5 whistles. Cool, puree and strain.
- Boil strained puree. Add Quaker Oats dissolved in ½ cup water.
- Add salt and pepper and simmer for 5 minutes.
- Serve hot.

*For powdered Quaker Oats, roast Quaker Oats for 2–3 minutes.
Cool and grind in a mixer.

Serves: 4

Recipe developed by cookery expert Smita Srivastava.

Quaker Oats & Broccoli Soup

Suggested garnishing.

Ingredients

- 3 tbsp Quaker Oats,* roasted and powdered
- 1 cup broccoli florets
- 4–5 garlic cloves, minced
- 3 cups of water
- ½ cup skimmed milk
- 1 onion, finely chopped
- 3 tbsp frozen / freshly steamed sweetcorn
- 2 drops of oil for sautèing
- Salt and pepper to taste

Preparation

- Blanch broccoli, strain and reserve water.
- Keep few aside and puree the rest.
- Heat 2 drops of oil and sautè garlic and onion.
- Add puree, blanched florets and reserved water.
- Add milk, sweetcorn, pepper and Quaker Oats dissolved in ½ cup water.
- Simmer for 5 minutes and serve hot.

*For powdered Quaker Oats, roast Quaker Oats for 2–3 minutes.
Cool and grind in a mixer.

Serves: 4

Recipe developed by cookery expert Smita Srivastava.

Quaker Oats & Spinach Masala Swirl

Suggested garnishing.

Ingredients

- ½ cup Quaker Oats
- ¾ cup hot water
- 1 cup ice-cold water
- 10–12 spinach leaves / ¼ cup blanched spinach
- 1½ cup low-fat yogurt
- 1 tsp roasted jeera powder
- Rock salt to taste
- ¼ tsp paprika (optional)
- Salt to taste

Preparation

- Soak Quaker Oats in hot water for 2–3 minutes. Mix to form a smooth mixture.
- Put the spinach leaves and soaked Quaker Oats in a blender and blend till smooth.
- Mix in yogurt, cold water and spices. Blend for another 30 seconds.
- Garnish with a dash of paprika and serve immediately.

Makes: 3 glasses

Recipe developed by cookery expert Smita Srivastava.

Notes:

Quaker Breakfast

Quaker Oats Dosa

Suggested garnishing.

◟ Ingredients

- 1 cup (100 gms) powdered Quaker Oats*
- ¼ cup (25 gms) powdered urad dal
- 1½ cups water (300 ml approx.)
- Salt to taste

Filling
- ½ onion – sliced, 1 green chilli – chopped, a few curry leaves
- 3 potatoes – boiled and mashed roughly
- ½ tsp brown mustard seeds (rai)
- 1 dry red chilli – broken into pieces
- Salt and red chilli powder to taste
- 1 tsp sambar powder

◟ Preparation

- Heat pan and add the dry red chilli and mustard seeds.
- When it crackles, add onions, curry leaves and green chillies.
- Cook on low heat till the onions turn soft.
- Add salt, red chilli powder, sambar powder and potatoes.
- Stir-fry for 2 – 3 minutes and keep aside.
- Mix Quaker Oats* powder, urad dal powder and salt with water in a vessel to obtain a thin pouring batter.
- Keep aside for 5 – 10 minutes till it becomes slightly thick.
- Heat a non-stick pan. Pour a ladle of batter on low flame, spreading from inside to get a round shape.
- When the edges turn brown, put some filling in the centre and fold over.
- Remove and serve with chutney.

*For powdered Quaker Oats, roast Quaker Oats for 2 – 3 minutes.
Cool and grind in a mixer.

Makes: 5–6 dosas

Recipe developed by cookery expert Nita Mehta.

Quaker Oats Idli

Suggested garnishing.

◟ Ingredients

- ½ cup powdered Quaker Oats*
- ½ cup semolina / suji
- ½ tsp baking powder
- 1 cup low-fat curd
- Salt to taste
- ½ cup water (approx.)

◟ Preparation

- Mix all the ingredients with water to make a thick but smooth batter.
- Keep aside for 10 minutes.
- Pour into the idli stands and steam for 10 – 15 minutes.

*For powdered Quaker Oats, roast Quaker Oats for 2 – 3 minutes.
Cool and grind in a mixer.

Serves: 8

Recipe developed by cookery expert Nita Mehta.

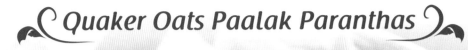

Quaker Oats Paalak Paranthas

Suggested garnishing.

Ingredients

For dough
- ½ cup (50 gms) powdered Quaker Oats*
- ½ cup wholewheat flour (atta)
- ¼ tsp carom seeds (ajwain)
- A pinch of salt
- ¼ cup skimmed milk

For filling
- 2 cups (100 gms) finely chopped spinach
- 1 tsp finely chopped ginger and garlic, ½ tsp chopped chilli
- 2 tsp low-fat curd
- 50 gms low-fat paneer – preferably home-made and mashed
- ¼ tsp salt to taste
- ⅛ tsp red chilli powder to taste

Preparation

- Mix the dough ingredients and make a soft dough with water. Cover and keep aside.
- Heat non-stick pan. Add ginger, garlic and chopped chilli, and stir.
- Add curd and sauté for 1 – 2 minutes. Add chopped spinach and cook on medium flame till dry.
- Add salt, red chilli powder and paneer. Dry-cook for 1 – 2 minutes. Remove from fire and allow to cool.
- Divide dough into 3 – 4 balls. Roll into a small flat circle, place filling in the center and close from all sides.
- Press over the dry flour and roll into medium-sized paranthas.
- Cook paranthas on medium heat, spreading 1 tbsp milk on both sides till brown patches appear.
- Serve hot.

*For powdered Quaker Oats, roast Quaker Oats for 2 – 3 minutes.
Cool and grind in a mixer.

Makes: 3

Recipe developed by cookery expert Nita Mehta.

Quaker Oats Upma

Ingredients

- 1 cup (100 gms) powdered Quaker Oats*
- ½ tsp mustard seeds (sarson)
- 1 dry red chilli
- 2 tbsp split gram dal (chane ki dal)
- 1 tsp split black beans (urad dal)
- 10 – 12 curry leaves – optional
- 1 onion, chopped finely
- 1 tomato, chopped
- 2 cups water
- Salt to taste
- ½ cup (50 gms) corn kernels, boiled or frozen
- ½ capsicum, chopped finely
- Juice of 1 lemon

Preparation

- Add mustard seeds, dry red chilli, chana dal, urad dal and curry leaves in a heated pan.
- Stir on low heat till the dal turns light brown. Add onions and stir till it turns soft.
- Add boiling water and salt. Cover and cook on low flame for 3 – 4 minutes.
- Add chopped tomato, capsicum and corn kernels.
- Now add Quaker Oats gradually with one hand, stirring with the other hand continuously.
- Stir-fry the upma for 2 – 3 minutes till dry. Turn off fire and add lemon juice. Mix well and serve.

*For powdered Quaker Oats, roast Quaker Oats for 2 – 3 minutes.
Cool and grind in a mixer.

Serves: 4

Recipe developed by cookery expert Nita Mehta.

Quaker Oats Spanish Omelette

๑ Ingredients

- 1 cup (100 gms) Quaker Oats
- Egg white from 4 eggs
- Salt to taste
- ½ tsp pepper
- 2 tbsp skimmed milk
- 1 small capsicum, finely sliced
- 1 small onion, finely sliced
- ½ small tomato, finely sliced
- 2 mushrooms, finely sliced (optional)

๑ Preparation

- Beat a mixture of egg white, Quaker Oats, salt, pepper and milk.
- On low flame, pour half of the egg mixture, and roll to cover the bottom of a non-stick pan.
- Sprinkle capsicum, onion, tomato and mushrooms on top and press gently.
- Cover the pan and cook for 1–2 minutes on low heat till the vegetables get steamed.
- Turn the side and cook till light golden. Make the other omelette with the remaining egg mixture.
- Serve with the vegetable side up. Cut into wedges, serve hot with toasted bread.

Serves: 4

Recipe developed by cookery expert Nita Mehta.

Notes:

Quaker Main Meals

Quaker Oats Dahi Bhalla

Suggested garnishing.

Ingredients

- 20 gms roasted and powdered Quaker Oats*
- 30 gms urad dal (white)
- 20 gms moong dal (white)
- ¼ tsp baking powder
- 200 gms low-fat curd
- Salt to taste
- ¼ tsp red chilli powder
- ¼ tsp roasted cumin (jeera) powder

Preparation

- Soak the urad and moong dals overnight in water.
- Grind them to a fine paste without water, and let it ferment for 3–4 hours.
- Add Quaker Oats* powder and whisk till light.
- Add baking powder. Mix well, pour in idli steamer and steam for 15–20 minutes.
- Soak bhalle in lukewarm water till soft and squeeze out the water.
- Add salt and water to the low-fat curd to get a thin consistency.
- Place the bhalle in low-fat curd and garnish with red chilli powder and jeera powder.

*For powdered Quaker Oats, roast Quaker Oats for 2–3 minutes.
Cool and grind in a mixer.

Serves: 3

Recipe developed by the Institute of Home Economics, New Delhi.

Quaker Oats Tomato Rice

⚬ Ingredients

- ¾ cup (75 gms) Quaker Oats, roasted
- ½ cup (50 gms) brown rice
- 1 tsp red chilli powder
- 2 large tomatoes, chopped finely
- 2 medium tomatoes, cut into 6 pieces
- 2 green chillies, slit
- 2 tbsp lemon juice
- Salt to taste

⚬ Preparation

- Cook the rice in 6 – 8 cups of water with a little salt for 7 – 8 minutes till the rice turns tender yet firm.
- Strain and keep aside to cool.
- Heat pan. Add chopped tomatoes. Cook for 4 – 5 minutes.
- Add salt, red chilli powder and green chillies.
- Add the larger pieces of tomatoes and cook for 1 – 2 minutes.
- Add roasted Quaker Oats and mix for 1 – 2 minutes.
- Add rice and mix. Add lemon juice and mix lightly.
- Serve hot.

Serves: 4

Recipe developed by cookery expert Nita Mehta.

Quaker Oats Papdi Chat

Ingredients

For papdi
- 20 gms roasted and powdered Quaker Oats*
- 20 gms wheat flour
- A pinch of salt

For meethi chutney
- 1 tsp amchoor powder
- 2 tsp sugar
- ¼ tsp salt
- ⅛ tsp red chilli powder
- ⅛ tsp jeera powder

For chat
- 75 gms (boiled and diced) potato
- 20 gms (soaked and boiled) chanas
- 150 gms low-fat curd
- 2 tsp meethi chutney
- Salt to taste
- ¼ tsp red chilli powder
- ¼ tsp roasted cumin seed powder

Preparation

For papdi
- Mix the atta, oats and salt to make a soft dough. Cover and keep for 5 minutes.
- Divide dough into small balls.
- Roll into papdi and bake in a moderately hot oven.

For chutney
- Boil amchoor powder, salt, red chilli powder, jeera powder with sugar in water.
- Cook till the chutney thickens. Remove from fire.

For chat
- Put the boiled and diced potatoes and chanas on papdi in a plate.
- Pour beaten curd over it. Top it with chutney.
- Serve with a sprinkling of salt, red chilli powder and roasted cumin seed powder.

*For powdered Quaker Oats, roast Quaker Oats for 2–3 minutes. Cool and grind in a mixer.

Serves: 2

Recipe developed by the Institute of Home Economics, New Delhi.

Quaker Oats & Paneer / Tofu Makhni

Suggested garnishing.

৵ Ingredients

- 10 gms roasted and powdered Quaker Oats*
- 50 gms low-fat paneer/tofu
- 1 small (50 gms) onion
- 5 gms ginger
- 2 cloves of garlic
- 1 small (50 gms) tomato (pureed)
- Salt to taste
- ¼ tsp red chilli powder
- ¼ tsp turmeric powder
- ¼ tsp garam masala powder
- 1 tsp oil

৵ Preparation

- Heat oil and add paste of onion, ginger and garlic. Fry till it turns light brown.
- Add tomato puree and fry for a few minutes. Add salt, red chilli powder and turmeric powder.
- Add water and cook on low flame for 5–7 minutes till the gravy thickens.
- Cut the tofu into triangles or squares and add with Quaker Oats* powder to the gravy.
- Simmer for a few minutes and serve garnished with garam masala and coriander leaves.

*For powdered Quaker Oats, roast Quaker Oats for 2–3 minutes.
Cool and grind in a mixer.

Serves: 1

Recipe developed by the Institute of Home Economics, New Delhi.

Quaker Oats & Tofu Manchurian

Suggested garnishing.

Ingredients

For fritters

- ½ cup lightly roasted Quaker Oats*
- 150 gms tofu
- 1 cup seasonal vegetables, finely chopped
- 2 tsp garlic, finely chopped
- Oil for brushing
- Salt, pepper and chilli to taste

For gravy

- 1 tsp finely chopped ginger and garlic
- 1 tsp cornflour dissolved in 2 tbsp water
- 1 tsp soy sauce
- ½ cup finely chopped seasonal vegetables
- Salt, pepper and vinegar to taste

Preparation

- Boil tofu in salted water for 3–4 minutes and crumble.
- Mix to fritter ingredients and shape into small balls.
- Brush with a little oil and bake till crisp.
- Heat a drop of oil in a non-stick pan. Sautè ginger, garlic and vegetables.
- Add 1½ cup water, salt, pepper, soy sauce, and boil.
- Mix in dissolved cornflour and simmer till thick. Add fritters and vinegar. Serve hot.

Serves: 4

Recipe developed by cookery expert Smita Srivastava.

Notes:

Quaker Snacks

Quaker Oats Dhokla

Ingredients

- 25 gms roasted and powdered Quaker Oats*
- 25 gms gram flour (besan)
- 75 gms curd (prepared from skimmed milk)
- 2.5 gms ginger, grated
- Salt to taste
- 1.5 gms oil
- ¼ tsp baking powder

Preparation

- Make a batter using Quaker Oats, curd and besan. Mix and keep aside for 1 hour.
- Add ginger, salt and baking powder and mix well.
- Grease a thali, pour dhokla batter in it and steam till done and set.
- Heat oil in a pan. Add mustard seeds, chopped green chillies and 2 tsp water.
- Pour over dhokla. Cut into square pieces and serve.

*For powdered Quaker Oats, roast Quaker Oats for 2–3 minutes.
Cool and grind in a mixer.

Serves: 2

Recipe developed by the Institute of Home Economics, New Delhi.

Quaker Oats Mushroom Croquettes

Suggested garnishing.

⚘ Ingredients

- ½ cup (50 gms) Quaker Oats
- 1 onion, chopped
- ½ cup finely chopped mushrooms
- ¾ cup (150 gms) skimmed milk, approx.
- Salt and pepper to taste
- 3 – 4 tbsp chopped green coriander
- 2 green chillies, chopped

⚘ Preparation

- Heat a non-stick pan. Add onion and sautè till light pink.
- Add mushrooms and sautè for 2 minutes.
- Add Quaker Oats and milk, stirring continuously. Cook till batter thickens and starts leaving the sides of the pan.
- Add salt and pepper. Remove from fire.
- Add coriander and chillies. Mix well and cool the mixture.
- Shape the mixture into 7 – 8 croquettes (oblong rolls with flat sides).
- Grill in oven or pan-fry for 10 – 15 minutes. Turn the side once after 5 minutes.
- Serve hot with ketchup and toasts.

Serves: 2–3

Recipe developed by cookery expert Nita Mehta.

Quaker Oats Litti

Ingredients

For litti
- 100 gms wheat flour
- 50 gms spinach
- A pinch of carom seeds (ajwain)
- Salt to taste

For filling
- 30 gms roasted Quaker Oats
- 25 gms onion
- ½ piece ginger
- 3 cloves of garlic
- 2 green chillies
- ½ lemon
- Salt to taste

Preparation

For filling
- Mix Quaker Oats with chopped onion, ginger, garlic, green chillies and salt.
- Add lemon juice and a little water to bind.

For litti
- Cook spinach till tender and then grind to a paste.
- Add salt and ajwain to the flour. Mix and make a soft dough with spinach paste and a little water.
- Keep dough covered for about 15 minutes.
- Divide the dough into 5 – 6 portions.
- Flatten each ball, put a spoonful of filling into it and shape into a ball again.
- Press lightly, using your palms to flatten it.
- Bake the prepared balls in a moderately hot oven.

Serves: 2

Recipe developed by the Institute of Home Economics, New Delhi.

Quaker Oats Namakparas

Suggested garnish

Ingredients

- 20 gms roasted and powdered Quaker Oats*
- 30 gms refined flour
- 5 gms oil
- Salt to taste

Preparation

- Add seasoning and roasted Quaker Oats* to maida. Rub in oil.
- Knead into a stiff dough using water.
- Roll the dough flat to 1/8" thickness and cut into namakpara shapes.
- Grease the baking tray and bake them till golden brown.
- Store in airtight jar.

*For powdered Quaker Oats, roast Quaker Oats for 2 – 3 minutes.
Cool and grind in a mixer.

Serves: 2

Recipe developed by the Institute of Home Economics, New Delhi.

Quaker Oats Creamy Mushrooms

Suggested garnishing.

Ingredients

- ½ cup Quaker Oats
- 1 grated garlic
- 1 finely chopped onion
- ½ cup finely chopped mushrooms
- 2 drops oil
- 1 cup skimmed milk
- ¼ tsp oregano
- Salt to taste

Preparation

- Heat oil in a non-stick pan and add onion, garlic and mushrooms and sautè till tender.
- Add milk, Quaker Oats, oregano and salt. Cook for 3 minutes.
- Sprinkle some pepper and chilli flakes and serve.

Recipe developed by cookery expert Smita Srivastava.

Notes:

Quaker Desserts

Quaker Oats Pear Crisp

Suggested garnishing.

Ingredients

- ¾ cup Quaker Oats
- 5 pears cut into small 2' pieces
- Sugar to taste
- ¼ cup finely chopped almonds
- 1 tbsp cornflour
- ¼ cup orange / apple juice
- 1 tbsp lemon juice

Preparation

- Pre-heat oven to 180°C.
- Toss pears with cornflour, 1 tbsp sugar and lemon juice.
- Mix Quaker Oats with 2 tbsp sugar, almonds and orange / apple juice.
- Put the pear mixture in a baking dish and top with Quaker Oats mixture.
- Bake for 30 minutes till the juices are thick and bubbling.
- Serve hot or warm.

Serves: **4**

Recipe developed by cookery expert Natasha Minocha.

Quaker Oats Mishti Doi

Suggested garnishing.

ꙮ Ingredients

- 5 tsp roasted and powdered Quaker Oats*
- 1 cup low-fat yogurt
- 3 tsp sugar
- 2 tsp caramelized sugar
- ¼ tsp vanilla flavour

ꙮ Preparation

- Whisk yogurt with sugar.
- Add powdered Quaker Oats* and vanilla flavour.
- Chill in refrigerator for 30 minutes.
- Serve with chopped fruits.

*For powdered Quaker Oats, roast Quaker Oats for 2–3 minutes.
Cool and grind in a mixer.

Serves: 2

Recipe developed by cookery expert Smita Srivastava.

Quaker Oats Banana / Mango Pancake

Ingredients

- ¾ cup (175 gms) powdered Quaker Oats*
- 1 banana or 1 ripe mango – sliced
- ¼ cup plain flour (maida)
- Egg white from 2 eggs
- ½ – ¾ cup (150 gms) skimmed milk
- Sugar to taste
- 1 tsp vanilla flavour

Preparation

- Puree the sliced banana or mango with little milk in a mixer.
- Add Quaker Oats* powder, plain flour, egg white, sugar, vanilla flavour and the remaining milk in the puree.
- Mix well to obtain a batter of pouring consistency.
- Heat a non-stick pan and pour 2 tbsp of the pancake batter, spreading it lightly like a dosa on low heat.
- Cover with a lid and cook for 2 minutes on medium flame.
- Once edges are brown, remove from fire and place on a plate.
- Spread with maple syrup or honey. Roll up and serve.

*For powdered Quaker Oats, roast Quaker Oats for 2–3 minutes. Cool and grind in a mixer.

Serves: 6

Recipe developed by cookery expert Nita Mehta.

Quaker Oats and Carrot Kheer

Ingredients

- 15 gms roasted Quaker Oats
- 300 ml skimmed milk
- 50 gms grated carrots
- 1 tsp sugar
- 1 green cardamom

Preparation

- Boil milk, add carrots, and let it simmer for 10 minutes.
- Add Quaker Oats and cook on slow fire, stirring continuously.
- When the kheer thickens to an even consistency, add sugar and green cardamom powder.
- Cook for a few more minutes, stirring constantly.
- Remove from fire and serve hot.

Serves: 1

Recipe developed by the Institute of Home Economics, New Delhi.

Quaker Oats Granola Parfait

Suggested garnishir

Ingredients

For granola
- 3 cups Quaker Oats
- ¼ cup pumpkin seeds
- ¼ cup sunflower seeds
- ½ cup sliced almonds
- ¼ cup flax seeds
- 1 tbsp vegetable oil
- ⅓ cup honey
- ⅓ cup water
- 1 scraped vanilla bean
- Salt to taste

For parfait
- ¾ – 1 cup granola
- 400 gms low-fat yogurt hung for at least 2 hours and chilled
- 1 tbsp icing sugar (can be substituted by honey)
- ¾ cup diced fresh seasonal fruit

Preparation

- Pre-heat oven to 150°C.
- Combine vegetable oil, honey, water, vanilla and salt in a small saucepan, and bring up to a simmer.
- Combine all dry ingredients in a bowl and add the liquid mixture to the dry ingredients.
- Mix well and transfer to the baking tray. Bake for about 45 minutes, stirring occasionally.
- Cool and transfer to an airtight container. Granola hardens further as it cools.

Method for parfait
- Lightly beat the hung yogurt with the sugar or honey till creamy.
- Take 2 small glasses. Layer first the yogurt, then fruit and then the granola.
- Repeat once more and top the glass generously with granola.
- Refrigerate for an hour before serving.

Serves: 2

Recipe developed by cookery expert Natasha Minocha.

Notes:

Quaker Shakes, Drinks and Smoothies

Quaker Oats Sattu

Suggested garnishin

Ingredients

- 20 gms roasted and powdered Quaker Oats*
- 30 gms sattu powder (10 gms wheat flour + 10 gms barley flour + 10 gms dry peas flour)
- Sugar to taste

Preparation

- Mix Quaker Oats* with sattu powder.
- Add water and sugar to the sattu mixture. Stir well.
- Serve chilled.

*For powdered Quaker Oats, roast Quaker Oats for 2 – 3 minutes. Cool and grind in a mixer.

Serves: 1

Recipe developed by the Institute of Home Economics, New Delhi.

Quaker Oats Lassi (Sweet)

Suggested garnishing

Ingredients

- 15 gms roasted and powdered Quaker Oats*
- 100 gms low-fat curd
- ½ cup water
- 1 tsp sugar

Preparation

- Blend curd, Quaker Oats*, sugar and water in a blender.
- Add the remaining water and crushed ice cubes and blend well.
- Pour in a tall glass and serve chilled.

[For salted lassi, instead of sugar, add salt to taste and jeera (cumin seeds) powder (⅛ tsp) along with a few mint leaves to garnish.]

*For powdered Quaker Oats, roast Quaker Oats for 2 – 3 minutes. Cool and grind in a mixer.

Serves: 1

Recipe developed by the Institute of Home Economics, New Delhi.

Quaker Oats Masala Buttermilk

Ingredients

- ½ cup Quaker Oats
- 1½ cup low-fat yogurt / curd
- ½-inch piece ginger
- ¼ cup mint leaves
- ¼ tsp cumin (jeera) powder
- ½ tsp sugar (optional)
- Black salt and green chillies to taste

Preparation

- Roast Quaker Oats for 4 – 5 minutes. Cool and grind.
- Soak Quaker Oats in ¾ cup hot water for 2 – 3 minutes.
- Blend mint leaves, chillies, ginger and soaked Quaker Oats till smooth.
- Add curd, spices and a cup of ice-cold water. Blend for 30 seconds.
- Garnish with mint and serve.

Makes: 3 glasses

Recipe developed by cookery expert Smita Srivastava.

Notes:

Quick & Easy
Savoury Quaker Oats

Quaker Oats Lemon Rice Style

Suggested garnishing.

Ingredients

- ½ cup Quaker Oats
- ¼ tsp mustard seeds
- 5–6 curry leaves
- ¼ tsp chana dal
- ¼ tsp turmeric powder
- 1 chopped green chilli, salt (to taste), half a lemon

Preparation

- Dry-roast the mustard seeds, chana dal and curry leaves in a pan.
- Add 1 cup water along with turmeric, green chilli and salt (to taste).
- Add Quaker Oats and cook for 2–3 minutes. Add the juice of the lemon, mix well and serve.

Recipe developed by cookery expert Smita Srivastava.

Quaker Oats in Tamarind Rasam Style

Suggested garnishing.

๙ Ingredients

- ½ cup Quaker Oats
- ¼ tsp mustard seeds
- A pinch of asafoetida powder
- 5 – 6 curry leaves
- 2 tsp ready-made tamarind pulp
- 1 finely chopped tomato
- 2 garlic cloves, finely minced
- ¼ tsp roasted cumin (jeera) powder
- ¼ tsp coriander powder
- 1 tbsp chopped coriander leaves
- Salt and pepper to taste

๙ Preparation

- Dry-roast the mustard seeds, asafoetida powder and 5 – 6 curry leaves in a pan.
- Boil 2 cups water, add tamarind pulp, tomato, garlic, jeera powder, coriander powder, coriander leaves, salt and pepper.
- Let it simmer for 2 minutes.
- Add Quaker Oats and cook for 3 minutes.
- Garnish with chopped green chilli and serve hot.

Recipe developed by cookery expert Smita Srivastava.

Quaker Oats with Leftover Curry

Suggested garnishing

Ingredients

- ½ cup Quaker Oats
- 1 cup leftover curry
- A pinch of garam masala
- 1 chopped chilli
- Salt (to taste)

Preparation

- Boil the leftover curry with ¼ cup water.
- Add Quaker Oats, garam masala, chilli and salt.
- Cook for 3 minutes.
- Garnish with coriander and serve hot.

Recipe developed by cookery expert Smita Srivastava.

Quaker Oats Curd Rice Style

Suggested garnishing

Ingredients

- ½ cup Quaker Oats
- ¼ tsp mustard seeds
- ¼ tsp urad dal
- 5 – 6 curry leaves
- Salt to taste
- ½ cup low-fat yogurt
- 1 green chilli – chopped for garnish

Preparation

- Dry-roast the mustard seeds, urad dal and curry leaves in a pan.
- Add ¾ cup water with Quaker Oats and salt. Cook for 2 – 3 minutes.
- Turn off the flame and whisk in yogurt.
- Garnish with green chillies and serve.

Recipe developed by cookery expert Smita Srivastava.

Quaker Oats with Spinach & Paneer

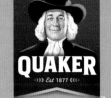

Ingredients

- ½ cup Quaker Oats
- ¼ cup skimmed milk
- 1 cup finely chopped spinach
- 2 cloves and 2 – 3 flakes minced garlic
- Chilli flakes
- A pinch of garam masala
- Julienned ginger and salt to taste
- ¼ cup crumbled low-fat paneer

Preparation

- Boil together ¾ cup water and milk.
- Add spinach, cloves and garlic and let simmer for 1 minute.
- Add Quaker Oats, chilli flakes, garam masala, julienned ginger and salt.
- Cook for 3 minutes. Remove from flame.
- Top with paneer and serve.

Recipe developed by cookery expert Smita Srivastava.

Notes:

Quaker Oats Plus
Multigrain Recipes

Quaker Oats Plus Uttapam

Suggested garnishing.

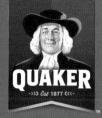

Ingredients

For Batter
- 1 cup (100 gms) Quaker Oats Plus
- ½ cup (50 gms) semolina / suji
- ¼ tsp asafoetida (hing) powder
- ½ tsp baking powder
- Salt to taste
- ¾ cup water (approx.)

For Topping
- ¼ cup grated carrots
- 1 onion, chopped
- 1 tomato, chopped
- ¼ cup boiled peas
- ¼ cup chopped cabbage
- 1–2 chopped green chillies
- ¼ tsp black pepper powder
- Curry leaves
- Salt to taste

Mix and keep aside.

Preparation

- Mix all batter ingredients to obtain a thick pouring consistency. Keep batter aside for ½ hour.
- Mix batter and pour 1 ladle on to a non-stick pan (on low flame).
- Spread batter (keep slightly thick) and sprinkle toppings and press lightly with a spoon to set.
- Cook till both sides are crisp and golden.

Serves: 3–4

Recipe developed by cookery expert Nita Mehta.

Quaker Oats Plus Stuffed Vegetables

Suggested garnishing.

Ingredients

- ½ cup roasted and powdered Quaker Oats Plus*
- 4 small capsicums
- 4 firm tomatoes
- ½ cup boiled and mashed potatoes
- ½ cup mashed cottage cheese (paneer)
- ½ cup shelled boiled peas
- 1 medium-sized onion, finely chopped
- 1 tsp coriander powder
- ½ tsp roasted cumin (jeera) powder
- ½ tsp chat masala
- ¼ tsp garam masala
- ½ tsp crushed garlic
- A few drops of lemon juice
- 2 tsp finely chopped green coriander
- 1 tsp chopped mint
- Salt and chilli powder to taste
- 1 tsp Quaker Oats Plus for topping

Preparation

- Clean and scoop seeds from capsicums and tomatoes.
- Grease non-stick pan and sautè onions turn pink.
- Add all ingredients and cook for 2 minutes and cool.
- Stuff mixture in vegetables and top with Quaker Oats Plus.
- Preheat oven. Bake at 200°C for 15 minutes or till tender.

*For powdered Quaker Oats Plus, roast Quaker Oats Plus for 2–3 minutes. Cool and grind in a mixer.

Makes: 4 tomatoes and 4 stuffed capsicums

Recipe developed by cookery expert Smita Srivastava.

Quaker Oats Plus Seekh Kebabs

Suggested garni

ᦞ Ingredients

For kebabs
- ¾ cup Quaker Oats Plus*, lightly roasted and powdered
- 1 cup rajma (kidney beans)
- ½ cup breadcrumbs (grind 2 slices of wholewheat bread in mixer)
- 2 large onions, finely chopped
- 1 large capsicum
- 2 small boiled and mashed potatoes
- 2 tbsp freshly ground ginger–garlic paste
- ½ tsp each of mango powder, garam masala and roasted cumin (jeera) powder
- Salt and chilli to taste
- Chat masala (optional)

For smoking and shaping
- A piece of coal
- 10 – 12 satay sticks / wooden skewers
- 2 tbsp Quaker Oats Plus for coating
- 2 drops of oil

ᦞ Preparation

- Soak rajma overnight, and boil, strain and mash to a smooth paste.
- Roast capsicum on open flame till charred. Peel, chop finely and mix with all the kebab ingredients.
- Keep a small steel bowl on a plate and place kebab mixture around it.
- Heat charcoal and place in the bowl, brush with 2 drops of oil.
- Cover and leave to smoke for 6 – 7 minutes.
- Shape mixture into seekh kebabs, roll over oats, brush oil lightly and grill till brown.
- Sprinkle chat masala and serve.

*For powdered Quaker Oats Plus, roast Quaker Oats Plus for 2 – 3 minutes. Cool and grind in a mixer.

Makes: 10–12 sticks

Recipe developed by cookery expert Smita Srivastava.

Quaker Oats Plus Falafels

Suggested garnishing.

Ingredients

- ½ cup roasted and powdered Quaker Oats Plus*
- ½ cup chickpeas (kabuli chana)
- 2 tbsp green gram (whole mung dal)
- 2 tbsp sweetcorn kernels
- 1 onion, finely chopped
- 3 – 4 garlic cloves, minced
- 4 tbsp finely chopped mint and coriander
- 1 tsp roasted cumin powder
- 1 tsp chat masala
- ½ cup breadcrumbs (grind 3 slices of wholewheat bread in a mixer)
- 1 tsp sesame seeds
- 1 pinch baking powder
- A few drops of oil for brushing
- Salt and chilli to taste

Preparation

- Soak chickpeas and beans for 6 – 8 hours. Drain and grind coarsely with mint, coriander and garlic.
- Add all ingredients and shape into 8 – 10 flat patties (tikkis).
- Brush with a drop of oil and grill / cook on a non-stick pan / tawa till crisp and golden.

*For powdered Quaker Oats Plus, roast Quaker Oats Plus for 2 – 3 minutes.
Cool and grind in a mixer.

Makes: 8–10 falafels

Recipe developed by cookery expert Smita Srivastava.

Quaker Oats Plus Instant Date Truffles

Suggested garnish

Ingredients

- 4 tsp roasted and powdered Quaker Oats Plus*
- ½ cup dates, pitted
- ¼ cup lightly roasted almonds and walnuts
- 2 tsp chopped raisins, figs and apricots
- 2 tsp skimmed milk, if required
- ¼ cup desiccated coconut for rolling

Preparation

- Grind the dates till pasty. Add coarsely ground nuts, Quaker Oats Plus*, milk and mix well.
- Shape into 7 – 8 balls. Roll in desiccated coconut. Serve.

(Can be refrigerated up to a week.)

*For powdered Quaker Oats Plus, roast Quaker Oats Plus for 2–3 minutes.
Cool and grind in a mixer.

Makes: 7–8 truffles

Recipe developed by cookery expert Smita Srivastava.

Notes: